LEARNING ADVENTURES
IN SCIENCE
Grades 1–2

By the Staff of Score@Kaplan

Foreword by Alan Tripp

Simon & Schuster

**This series is dedicated to our
Score@Kaplan parents and children—
thank you for making these books possible.**

Published by
Kaplan Educational Centers and Simon & Schuster
1230 Avenue of the Americas
New York, NY 10020

Special thanks to: Elissa Grayer, Doreen Beauregard, Julie Schmidt, Rebecca Geller
Schwartz, Linda Lott, Janet Cassidy, Marlene Greil, Nancy McDonald, Sarah Jane
Bryan, Chris Wilsdon, Janet Montal, Jeannette Sanderson, David Stienecker, Dan
Greenberg, Kathy Wilmore, Dorrie Berkowitz, Brent Gallenberger, and Molly Walsh

Head Coach and General Manager, Score@Kaplan: Alan Tripp
President, Score@Kaplan: Robert L. Waldron
Series Content and Development: Mega-Books
Project Editor: Mary Pearce
Production Editor: Donna Mackay, Graphic Circle Inc.
Art Director: Elana Goren-Totino
Illustrators: Rick Brown, Ryan Brown, Sandy Forrest, Larry Nolte,
Evan Polenghi, Fred Schrier, Peter Spacek, Arnie Ten
Cover Design: Cheung Tai
Cover Photograph: Michael Britto

Manufactured in the United States of America
Published Simultaneously in Canada

January 1998
10 9 8 7 6 5 4 3 2 1

ISBN:0-684-84426-5

Contents

Grade One

Grade Two

Dear Parents,

Your child's success in school is important to you, and at Score@Kaplan we are always pleased when the kids who attend our educational centers do well on their report cards. But what we really want for our kids is not just good grades. We also want everything that good grades are supposed to represent:

- We want our kids to master the key communication systems that make civilization possible: language (spoken and written), math, the visual arts, and music.
- We want them to build their critical-thinking skills so they can understand, appreciate, and improve their world.
- We want them to continually increase their knowledge and to value learning as the key to a happy, successful life.
- We want them to always do their best, to persist when challenged, to be a force for good, and to help others whenever they can.

These are ambitious goals, but our children deserve no less. We at Score@Kaplan have already helped thousands of children across the country in our centers, and we hope this series of books for children in first through sixth grades will reach many more households.

Simple Principles

We owe the remarkable success of Score@Kaplan to a few simple principles. This book was developed with these principles in mind.

- We expect every child to succeed.
- We make it possible for every child to succeed.
- We reinforce every instance of success, no matter how small.

Assessing Your Child

One helpful approach in assessing your child's skills is to ask yourself the following questions.

- How much is my child reading? At what level of difficulty?
- Has my child mastered appropriate language arts skills, such as spelling, grammar, and syntax?
- Does my child have the ability to express appropriately complex thoughts when speaking or writing?
- Does my child demonstrate mastery of all age-appropriate math skills, such as mastery of addition and subtraction facts, multiplication tables, division rules, and so on?

These questions are a good starting place and may give you new insights into your child's academic situation.

What's Going on at School

Parents will always need to monitor the situation at school and take responsibility for their child's learning. You should find out what your child should be learning at each grade level and match that against what your child actually learns.

The activity pages in *Learning Adventures* were developed using the standards developed by the professional teachers associations. As your child explores the activities in *Learning Adventures*, you might find that a particular concept hasn't been taught in school or hasn't yet been mastered by your child. This presents a great opportunity for both of you. Together you can learn something new.

Encouraging Your Child to Learn at Home

This book is full of fun learning activities you can do with your child to build understanding of key concepts in language arts, math, and science. Most activities are designed for your child to do independently. But that doesn't mean that you can't work on them together or invite your child to share the work with you. As you help your child learn, please bear in mind the following observations drawn from experience in our centers:

- Positive reinforcement is the key. Try to maintain a ratio of at least five positive remarks to every negative one.
- All praise must be genuine. Try praises such as: "That was a good try," "You got this part of it right," or "I'm proud of you for doing your best, even though it was hard."
- When a child gets stuck, giving the answer is often not the most efficient way to help. Ask open-ended questions, or rephrase the problem.
- Remember to be patient and supportive. Children need to learn that hard work pays off.

There's More to Life Than Academic Learning

Most parents recognize that academic excellence is just one of the many things they would like to ensure for their children. At Score@Kaplan, we are committed to developing the whole child. These books are designed to emphasize academic skills and critical thinking, as well as provide an opportunity for positive reinforcement and encouragement from you, the parent.

We wish you a successful and rewarding experience as you and your child embark upon this learning adventure together.

Alan Tripp
General Manager
Score@Kaplan

Dear Kids,

This is your very own book of Learning Adventures.
It has puzzles, games, riddles, and lots of other fun things for
you to do.
You can do the activities alone.
Or you can share them with your family and friends.

If you get stuck on something, look for the Score coaches.
They will help you.
You can check the answers on pages 65-70, too.

We know you will do a great job.
That's why we have a special puzzle inside.
After you do three or four pages, you'll see a puzzle piece.
Cut it out.
Then glue it or tape it in place on page 64.
When you are done with the book, the puzzle will be done, too.
Then you'll find a secret message from us.

Go for it!

Your Coaches at Score

NAME_____

Be a Scientist!

Scientists get ideas and try them out.
Then they watch what happens.
You can be a scientist!
Try out ideas for making music.

What you need:
- 2 or 3 rubber bands
- shoe box
- 2 pots
- 2 pot lids
- spoon

Need ideas? Look at the instruments. How could you use your materials to make things like them?

What you do:
1. Look at your materials. Think of ways you could use them to make music. Draw your ideas here:

2. Now try out each idea.
3. Draw a picture of the idea that worked best.

Around the House: Ask your family members to help you think of more ways you could make music. Then try out your ideas!

NAME _____

Compare Fair

Astronaut I. M. Spacy brought a space
creature back from his latest trip!
Now he needs your help.
Look at the creature and the child.
How are they both alike?
Circle each thing you find in both pictures.

Around the House: Look at a friend or a brother
or sister. (They are a little like space creatures, right?)
Then look at yourself. How are the two of you alike?
How are you different?

NAME

Nature Walk

Good scientists use all their senses to find out about the world around them.
Look at the picture below.
Pretend you are there.
Then write what you would see, hear, smell, and touch.

I see _____

I hear _____

I smell _____

I touch _____

Around the House: Take a walk with a family member. Talk about what you see, hear, smell, and touch on your walk.

NAME _____

Surprise!

Do you know words for colors, shapes,
and sizes?
Find out.
Follow the directions to color the picture.

This is a *triangle*.
This is a *square*.
This is a *circle*.
This is a *rectangle*.

1. Find the large triangle. Color it red.
2. Find the two small squares. Color them blue.
3. Find the small triangle. Color it orange.
4. Find the large square. Color it purple.
5. Find the four rectangles. Color them green.
6. Find the four small circles. Color them yellow.
7. Draw a smile. Color it any color you like.

NAME_____

Toys or Tools?

Scientists need to put like things together.
So does Jack when he cleans his room.
You can help Jack.
Draw a line from each object to the box it goes in.

Now think of another thing to put in each box.
Draw a picture of it.
Then draw a line from the thing to the right box.

Check Yourself: Did you put the same number of things in each box? If not, try again.

NAME _____

Is It Alive?

Can you tell if something is living?
Look at each picture.
Color all the living things red.
Color all the nonliving things blue.

Did you know that plants, animals, and people are all living things?

Nice Job! Now cut out the puzzle piece. Glue or tape it in the right place on page 64.

Around the House: What living things are in your home? What nonliving things are in your home? Show each thing to a family member.

6

Grade 1

Measure Up

Scientists need tools to measure things.
Look at each tool below.
Draw a line to match each tool to the words
that tell what it measures.

1.
ruler

    a. weight
(how heavy something is)

2.
scale

    b. height or length
(how tall or long something is)

3.
measuring cup

    c. volume
(how much of something there is)

You can use your hand as a measuring tool.
How many hands long:

4. Is your leg?_____

5. Is your shoe?_____

6. Is your bed?_____

7. Is this page?_____

Around the House: Look for a ruler, a scale, and a
measuring cup at your house. Ask a family member to
show you how to use them.

NAME _____

Food Maker

Plants use sunlight to make their own food.
What happens if a plant has no sun?
You can find out.

Plants need to eat just like you do. They need sun, water, and soil to make their food.

What you need:
- a plant or tree with leaves
- a small piece of black paper
- a paper clip

What you do:
1. Clip the paper onto a leaf.
2. Wait four days.
3. Take the paper off the leaf.

What you see:
Draw a picture that shows what the leaf looks like after four days.

What you think:
What would happen to a plant if all its leaves were covered up? Write a sentence that tells what you think. _____

_____

_____

8

NAME_____

We're Thirsty

People, plants, and animals need water to live.
But they get water in different ways.
Look at each row of pictures.
Color the picture in each row that shows the
way the living thing gets water.

1. People

2. Plants

3. Animals

Good work.
Now cut out
your puzzle
piece. Glue or
tape it in place
on page 64.

Around the House: Do you have plants or
animals in your house? Draw pictures to show how they
get water.

NAME

Where Does It Live?

Look at the plants and animals.
Can you figure out where each one lives?
Find all plants and animals that live in a
forest.
Color them green.
Find all plants and animals that live in an
ocean.
Color them blue.

Think! Which
of these
plants and
animals can
live under
water?

fish   pine tree   seaweed   bear   lobster

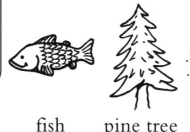  

sea anemone   raccoon   oak tree   starfish   blueberry
bushes

squirrel   bird   crab   deer   coral

Around the House: Look around your habitat.
Draw pictures of the plants and animals (including
people) that live there.

Life Science

Identify the effects
of living things
on the
environment

NAME_____

Help the Earth!

It's important to keep the earth clean.
Look at the picture below.
Pretend you are there.
Then write sentences that tell what you would
do to help clean up.

_____

_____

_____

_____

Around the House: Look around your backyard
or local park. Could it be cleaner? Talk with a family
member about planning a clean-up day.

NAME

How Do Seeds Grow?

Tasha planted a seed.
Then she drew pictures to show what happened.
Now her pictures are mixed up.
Number the pictures to show the right order.

A. ☐

B. ☐

C. ☐

D. ☐

12

Keep Them Growing

Jackie planted a flower garden.
Look at the picture of her garden.
Then answer the questions.

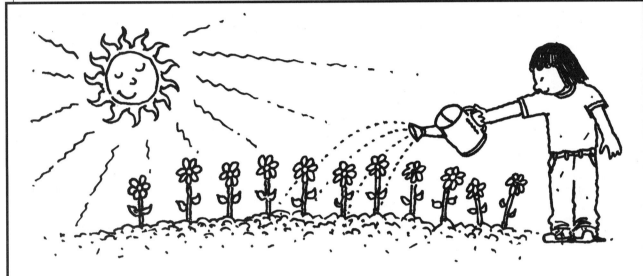

1. Where did Jackie plant her seeds? _____

_____

2. Why do you think Jackie put her garden outdoors? _____

_____

3. What is Jackie giving to the plants? _____

_____

4. What do the plants need to grow? _____

_____

Around the House: Think about having your
own flower garden. Draw a picture of it. Show where
your garden would be. Show where you would plant
each kind of flower.

13

NAME _____

Look-Alike Animals

Some plants and animals living today look like plants and animals that disappeared long ago.
The plants and animals on the left are alive today.
Draw a line to match each one to its look-alike from long ago on the right.

Over many, many years plants and animals change. They change in ways that help them survive better.

Animals Today		Animals in the Past	
elephant		ankylosaurus	
tiger		woolly mammoth	
ostrich		triceratops	
armadillo		saber-toothed tiger	
rhinoceros		struthiomimus	

14

NAME_____

It's So-oo Hot!

Heat can change food.
Look at each food on the left.
Then find the picture on the right that shows
how heat can change it.
Draw a line to match the pictures.

1.   A.

2.   B.

3.    C.

4.   D.

5.   E.

6.   F.

NAME _____

Hot Stuff

Kevin knew that water froze when it became very cold.
Then he wondered what would happen to water when it became very hot.
So he decided to try an experiment.
Ask an adult to help you try his experiment.

What you need:
- water
- ice cube tray
- pan

What you do:
1. Put some water in the ice cube tray. Put the tray in the freezer.
2. Wait about 3 hours. Then take the tray out of the freezer.
3. Draw a picture to show what happened to the water.
4. Now put the contents of the ice cube trays into the pan. Ask an adult to put the pan on the stove and turn the stove on.
5. Wait about 15 minutes.
6. Draw a picture to show what happened.
7. What happens to water when it becomes very hot?

_____
_____

16

NAME_____

Push or Pull?

Look at the toys.
Think about how they can move.
Color the toys you can push blue.
Color the toys you can pull red.
Color the toys you can push and pull yellow.

A push or pull can start, stop, or change the direction an object is moving in.

Awesome! Now cut out your piece and put it in place on page 64.

1.

2.

3.

4.

5.

6.

7.

8.

Check Yourself: Try to find each of the toys in your house. Test them to see whether you can push or pull them. Then check your answers above.

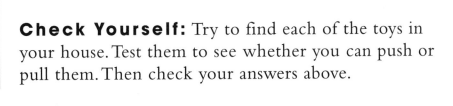

NAME _____

Fun With Sound

A *vibration* is a back-and-forth motion.
All sounds are made by vibrations.
Find out more about vibrations and sound by
doing this experiment.

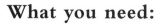

Thin bands vibrate quickly.

Thick bands vibrate more slowly.

What you need:
- 4 rubber bands of different thicknesses
- 2 pencils or markers
- baking pan or shoe box

What you do:

1. Stretch the rubber bands around the pan.
2. Pluck each band. Listen to the sound. What kind of sound do the thin bands make?

_____

What kind of sound do the thick bands make?

_____

3. Put a pencil under the rubber bands at each end.
4. Pluck each band again. Listen to the sound it makes. How did the sound change?

_____

_____

Around the House: Go on a sound hunt. Tap on different objects with a pencil. Find things that make a high sound and things that make a low sound.

Categories

Can you tell how things are alike?
Look at the different objects.
Then draw them in the boxes to show where
they belong.

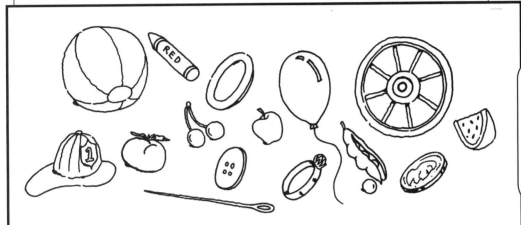

Remember,
some objects
might fit into
more than one
category or
group.

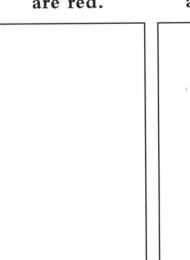

These objects are red.	These objects are round.	These objects are small.

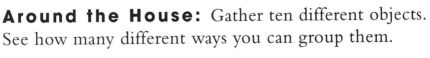

Around the House: Gather ten different objects.
See how many different ways you can group them.

NAME _____

Can You Find It?

One thing in each group does not belong.
Can you find it?
Color it.
Then write words that tell how the other
three things are alike.

Soft, hard, smooth, and *rough* are words that describe how things feel.

Now can you find where this puzzle piece belongs? Glue or tape it in place on page 64.

1.

   ribbon   glass   road   marbles

   _____

2.

   pillow   teddy bear   coat   car

   _____

3.

   ball   brush   mat   rose

   _____

4.

   stone column   nails   blanket   rock

   _____

NAME_____

Sink or Swim

Some objects float in water.
Other objects sink.
You can find out which objects float and
which ones sink by doing an experiment.

What you need:
- 6 small objects such as a plastic spoon, paper clip, button, plastic cup, piece of aluminum foil, and a coin
- a pan of water

What you do:
1. Write the name of each object in the chart below.
2. Make a guess about each object. Will it sink or float? Write **S** for sink or **F** for float in the chart.
3. Put each object in the water.
4. Does it sink or float? Write **S** for sink or **F** for float in the chart.

Object	What I think will happen	What really happened

NAME _____

What's the Attraction?

Nashila is trying to pick up objects with her magnet.
Decide which objects her magnet will pick up.
Circle your answers.
Do you have a magnet and some of the objects Nashila has?
If so, test each object.
If not, use what you know about magnets to help you decide.

A *magnet* is a special metal. It *attracts*, or pulls, other metals, such as iron.

Around the House: Look for magnets in your kitchen. You might find one stuck to the refrigerator or inside the kitchen cabinets. How are they used?

NAME_____

Moving Right Along

Get a long rubber band.
Then find the different ways you can make
it move.
Just follow each direction.
(We gave you a hint for the first one.)

1. Find a way to make the
rubber band move in a
circle. Then draw a picture
of what you did. (Hint: Put
the rubber band on your
finger. Twirl it around.)

2. Find a way to make the
rubber band move in a
straight line. Draw a
picture of what you did.

3. Find a way to make the
rubber band *vibrate,* or
move quickly back and
forth, like a guitar string.
Then draw a picture of
what you did.

Around the House: How many different ways can
you move? Can you move in a circle, move in a straight
line, and vibrate?

NAME _____

Seasons Come and Go

Can you tell what's wrong with each picture?
Look at each picture.
Decide which season it shows.
Write the name of the season on the line.
Then circle the things in each picture that do not belong.

There are four seasons: winter, spring, summer, and fall.

The coldest season is winter; the hottest season is summer.

Excellent! Now cut out the puzzle piece. Glue or tape it in place on page 64.

1.

_____

2.

_____

3.

_____

4.

_____

Around the House: The seasons don't always look the same in different parts of the country. Draw pictures that show what the seasons look like where you live.

NAME_____

How's the Weather?

Keep your own weather calendar for four days.
Write the name of each day on the lines in
the first row.
What is the weather on each day?
Write words and draw pictures in the chart.
Then draw a picture that shows how you
dressed for the weather.

Words and Pictures to Use				
cold cool	warm hot			
Day	1. _____	2. _____	3. _____	4. _____
weather				
how I dressed				

Earth and Space

Recognize the sun
as a source of
heat and light

NAME

Sunlight, Sun Hot!

It's a hot day, and Harry wants to keep cool.
Should he sit in a sunny place or a shady place?
Help Harry decide by doing this experiment.
Then answer the questions below.

What you need:
- 2 paper cups
- 2 ice cubes
- marker

What you do:
1. Label one cup *Sun* and the other cup *Shade.*
2. Put one ice cube in each cup.
3. Put the *Sun* cup outside in the sun. Put the *Shade* cup outside in the shade.
4. Wait 10 minutes. Then look at both cups. Draw a picture in the space below to show what happened to each ice cube.

5. Is there more heat in the sun or the shade? Why do you think so?_____

_____

6. Where should Harry go to keep cool on a hot day? Why do you think so?_____

_____

Shade is an area away from the sun.

NAME_____

Really Rockin'

Help Rockin' Rory describe the rocks in his collection.
Pick three words from the box to describe each rock.
Write the words below each picture.

| big small smallest dark light |
| darkest rough lightest |
| smooth smoothest |

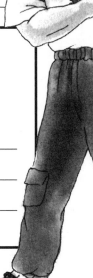

A rock is a small piece of the earth's crust.

_____
_____
_____

Now go outside and find your own rock.
Draw it in the space below.
Then write three words that describe it.

_____
_____
_____

NAME _____

Dinosaur Match

Read the sentences.
Then look at the pictures of the dinosaurs on the next page.
Use the information from the sentences and the pictures to name the dinosaurs.
Write the name on the blank.

1. My name means "king tyrant lizard."
    I have claws on my three toed feet.
    I am very strong, but I have small front legs.
    My mouth is filled with 6-inch-long sharp teeth.
    I am a meat eater.

    I am a _____ .

2. My name means "ostrich imitator."
    I have a bill like an ostrich, and I don't have any teeth.
    I can snap up insects and worms with my beak.
    I can run fast because of my long thin legs.

    I am a _____ .

3. My name means "stiff lizard."
    I am covered with a bumpy armor.
    I hide beneath it to protect myself.
    I also use my thick tail to strike out.
    I have blunt teeth, and I am a plant eater.

    I am a _____ .

4. I move slowly because I am so big.
    I have weak teeth, so I eat soft plants.
    My long neck helps me munch on leaves.
    I have nostrils on the top of my head.

    I am a _____ .

NAME_____

A. tyrannosaurus rex

B. brachiosaurus

Dinosaurs lived on Earth a long time ago, before people. There are no more dinosaurs. They are *extinct*.

Fossils are the remains of plants and animals that lived long ago. Scientists called *paleontologists* study dinosaur fossils to find out about dinosaurs.

C. ankylosaurus

D. struthiomimus

Technology

Identify objects
found in nature
and those made
by people

NAME _____

Maisie's Maze

**Help Maisie find her way through the maze.
Look at each object along the path.
Draw a line that connects only those objects
found in nature.**

These things were
made by nature.

These things were
made by people.

Way to go!
Now put the
puzzle piece in
place on page 64.

Around the House: Look around your backyard
for something found in nature. Then find something you
made. How are the two things different?

30

NAME_____

Computer ID

Read each sentence below.
Fill in each blank with a word from the box.
Then find and circle the words in the puzzle.
One is done for you.

monitor	printer	disk drive	software
keyboard	mouse	machine	

Computers are machines that can be used to do many things. People use computers at home, in school, and at work. You can do work on a computer or play a game. Computers can help people do some things faster than they could do them without a computer.

1. A computer is a ____machine____ .

2. Programs that run on your computer are called _____ .

3. You put a disk into the _____ .

4. You see your work on the _____ .

5. To move around the screen, you use the _____ .

6. The part you type on is the _____ .

7. The machine you use to print your work on paper is called a _____ .

```
A  B  C  D  E  F  G  H  P
M  O  N  I  T  O  R  I  J  R
A  S  K  S  M  Y  Z  A  B  I
C  C  L  K  O  O  C  D  E  N
H  R  M  D  U  X  B  F  G  T
I  E  N  R  S  V  W  S  T  E
N  E  O  I  E  N  L  K  E  R
E  N  P  V  O  P  M  L  J  Q
Q  R  K  E  Y  B  O  A  R  D
S  O  F  T  W  A  R  E  E  R
```

NAME _____

Way to Go

Think about all the ways you can travel. Draw a picture in each box to show how you can travel on land, on water, and in the air. Then write where you would go using each kind of transportation.

Transportation is how people and things get from one place to another.

You're a great traveler! Now cut out the puzzle piece. Glue or tape it in place on page 64.

On Land

_____
_____
_____
_____

On Water

_____
_____
_____
_____
_____

In the Air

_____
_____
_____
_____

NAME_____

Long Ago and Today

How can you travel today?
How would you have traveled if you lived
long ago?
Circle the ways you travel today.
Draw an X on the ways people traveled
long ago.

Around the House: Do you have great
grandparents or know very old people? Ask them how
they traveled when they were kids. How was it like
traveling today? How was it different?

NAME _____

Get the Fever!

Read the thermometers below.
Draw a happy face if the temperature is normal.
Draw a sick face if the temperature is too high or too low.
Write on the line whether the temperature is too high, too low, or O.K.
The first one is done for you.

A normal body temperature is 98.6°. A temperature above or below 98.6 means that you might be sick.

Hot stuff! Now cut out the puzzle piece. Glue or tape it in place on page 64.

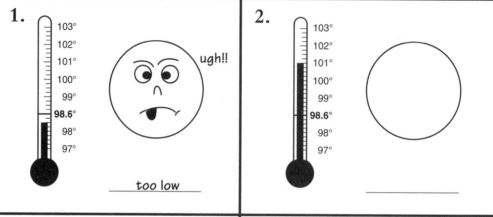

1. 103° 102° 101° 100° 99° **98.6°** 98° 97°   ugh!!

too low

2. 103° 102° 101° 100° 99° **98.6°** 98° 97°

_____

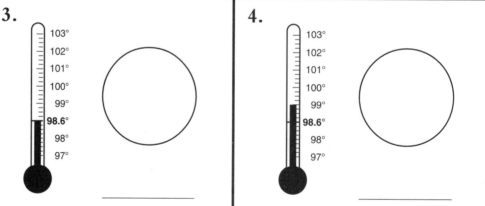

3. 103° 102° 101° 100° 99° **98.6°** 98° 97°

_____

4. 103° 102° 101° 100° 99° **98.6°** 98° 97°

_____

Around the House: Ask your parents for a thermometer. Take your temperature to see if it is normal.

To Freeze or Not to Freeze

The ocean near Maria's house doesn't freeze in winter.
But the lakes do.
Maria wondered why.
She thought it might be because the ocean is salty.
So she made up an experiment, or a test, to find out.
Do Maria's experiment below.

What you need:
- 2 paper cups full of water
- 2 teaspoons of salt
- spoon
- pen or marker

What you do:
1. Mix the salt into one cup of water.
   Put a mark on that cup.
2. Put both cups in the freezer.
   Wait about 2 hours.
3. After 2 hours, take the cups out of the freezer.
4. Draw a picture to show what happened.
5. Was Maria right? Did salt do anything to the water in the freezer? If so, what?_____

_____

_____

_____

Around the House: Ask a family member to help you with Maria's experiment. What did you find out?

NAME _____

Sense It

Scientists use words that tell about how things feel and smell.
Look at the pictures below.
Draw a line from each picture to all the words that tell about it.

smoky

rough

soft

hard

smooth

Around the House: Go on a hunt at your house. Find something soft. Find something bumpy. Find something that smells sweet. Then ask family members to close their eyes. Give them the objects and see if they can guess what they are.

Check Out the Map

Mia drew a map of her yard.
It shows where each thing is.
Use Mia's map to follow the directions below.

A *map* is a special kind of picture. It shows where things are. To make a map, pretend you are a bird looking down at a place. Then draw what you would see.

1. Find the flowers. Put an X on them.
2. Find the place where Mia can eat lunch. Color it brown.
3. Find the place where Mia can build a sand castle. Circle it.
4. Mia walked from the swings to the clubhouse. Then she walked to the garden. Draw a line to show where Mia walked.

Around the House: Make a map of your bedroom. Show its shape. Then show where each thing is. Share the map with family members. Could they use it to find things in your room?

NAME _____

Whose Job Is It?

Scientists use charts to help them remember things.
Kareem is making a chart, too.
Help him finish his family job chart.
Follow the directions below.

A *chart* can show information in a way that is easy to read.

Now your job is to put this puzzle piece on page 64. Glue or tape it in place.

walk dog	Kareem
set table	Jamal
clear table	Dwayne
wash dishes	

1. Add *dry dishes* and to the chart.
2. Kareem's little brother Jamal can't read. Draw a picture in each job box so Jamal can understand it.
3. Kareem and Dwayne can do all the jobs. But Jamal is too little for some jobs. Add one more job. Then give each boy the job that is right for him. Write the names in the chart.

What's Happening?

Li made a calendar.
It shows what he does after school.
Read his calendar.
Then answer the questions.

Monday	Tuesday	Wednesday	Thursday	Friday
piano lessons	play date	scout meeting	soccer practice	

A *calendar* can show days, weeks, or months in a year. It helps people remember when things will happen.

1. What does Li do on Monday?_____

2. If Li has a scout uniform on, what day is it?

3. What do you think Li might do on Friday? Draw it in the chart.

Around the House: Make a calendar to show what you do each day of the week. Put it up in your room to help you remember.

NAME _____

What Sally Saw

Sally has a science log.
She uses it to write down what she sees and does.
Look at one page from her log.
Then answer the questions.

Good scientists write information in *logs*, or journals. They help scientists remember things they see or do.

Date	What I Did or Saw	What I Learned
Thursday, March 4	I saw a bird making a nest.	Birds make their own homes.

1. When did Sally write in her log? _____

2. What did she see? _____

3. What did she learn? _____

4. How do you think the log helps Sally? _____

_____

_____

Way to go! Cut out your puzzle piece and put it in place on page 64.

Around the House: Make your own science log. Write or draw what you see and do. Write about what you learn. Then share it with your family.

NAME

Dinner Time!

Animals need to eat for energy, just like you.
Find three clues about each animal.
Color each animal's clues a different color.
Follow the trail to learn what each animal
likes to eat.

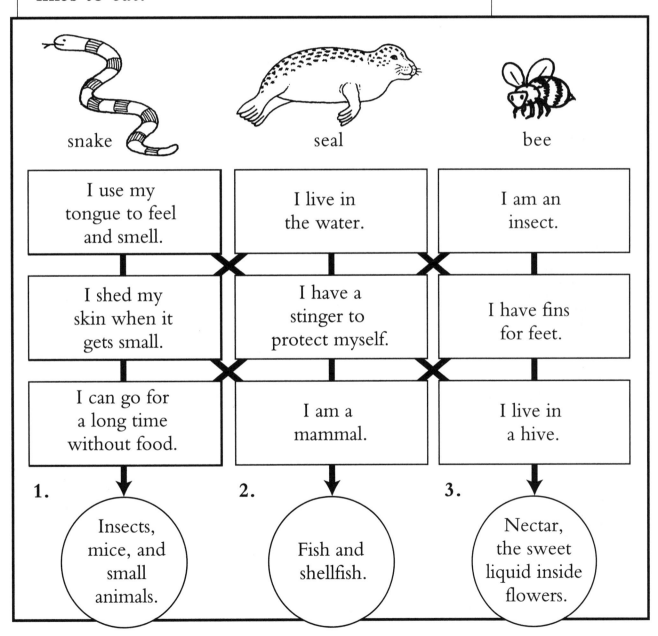

snake   seal   bee

I use my tongue to feel and smell.	I live in the water.	I am an insect.
I shed my skin when it gets small.	I have a stinger to protect myself.	I have fins for feet.
I can go for a long time without food.	I am a mammal.	I live in a hive.

1. Insects, mice, and small animals.

2. Fish and shellfish.

3. Nectar, the sweet liquid inside flowers.

NAME _____

Desert Riddles

Do you know what lives in a desert?
You will after you answer the riddles.
Read each riddle.
Find the answer in the box.
Write it on the line.

A *habitat* is a place where plants and animals live.

It doesn't rain much in the desert. The animals and plants need very little water to live.

| cactus | coyote | rattlesnake | sagebrush |

1. I am a plant. My insides are like a sponge. They can hold lots of water, so I can live with very little rain. If you touch me, you might get pricked.

   I am a _____ .

2. I get my name from my tail. It rattles when I move. I sleep in my hole in the day to stay cool. At night I come out to eat lizards and other small animals.

   I am a _____ .

3. I look something like a wolf. I hunt at night.

   I am a _____ .

4. I am one of the few woody plants that can grow in a desert. Long ago, people burned me in their fires because there are few trees in the desert.

   I am a _____ .

Around the House: Show the pictures to someone in your family. Read the names of the plants and animals together.

NAME_____

Don't Break the Chain

Look at the food chain.
It shows how animals use plants and other
animals for food.
Now read each riddle below.
Write a word from the food chain to answer
the riddle.

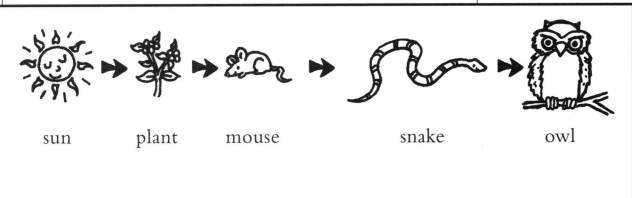

sun   plant   mouse   snake   owl

1. I am little, so I can hide where snakes can't get me.
   What am I?_____

2. I fly through the trees. I look for snakes to gobble up.
   What am I?_____

3. I grow in the ground. I use sunlight to make my food.
   What am I?_____

4. I keep an eye out for fat little mice. I swallow my food whole.
   What am I?_____

Around the House: What do you eat? Draw a
food chain that shows you at the end. Share your food
chain with family members.

NAME _____

Mike's Zoo!

Mike wants to make a zoo.
He has to put the animals where they belong.
Look at the animals on page 45.
Then draw each one in the correct part of
the zoo.

NAME_____

Birds have wings and feathers. *Reptiles* have scales and crawl on the ground.

Mammals have hair or fur. *Fish* have scales and live in the water.

Around the House: Look around your backyard or a nearby park. What animals do you see? Make a list. Then write whether each is a mammal, a bird, a reptile, or a fish.

NAME _____

Mothers and Babies

The baby animals need to find their mothers. You can help.
Draw a line from each baby to its mother.
Then follow the directions below.

When baby animals are born, they may not look exactly like their mothers. But you can usually tell which baby animal belongs to which mother.

1. Tell one way in which the babies look different from their mothers. _____

   _____

2. Tell one way in which the babies look the same as their mothers. _____

   _____

Here's your next piece of the puzzle. Put it in the right spot on page 64.

Around the House: Think about you and your mom or dad. How are you alike? How are you different?

NAME

What's the Difference?

Look at the pictures of the two people below.
How are they alike?
How are they different?
Use the pictures to fill in the chart below.
Put a check (√) next to the words that
describe each person.

	Man	Boy
male		
female		
tall		
short		
curly hair		
straight hair		
dark hair		
light hair		
freckles		
no freckles		
glasses		
no glasses		

Around the House: Make a chart to compare the
people in your family. How are they alike? How are they
different?

NAME _____

It's Electric!

Have you ever brushed your hair and had it stick to the brush?
That's caused by static electricity.
See what else static electricity does.
Look at the pictures, and read the sentences.
Answer the question by circling the picture on the right that shows what will probably happen.

Some objects are charged with electricity when they are rubbed with other objects. This is called *static electricity*. The electric charge pulls things toward it.

Awesome! Now cut out your puzzle piece. Find the right spot for it on page 64.

1.

Kyle takes off his sweater. What will probably happen?

a.

b.

2.

Keesha holds a balloon next to paper. What will probably happen?

a.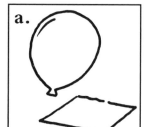

b.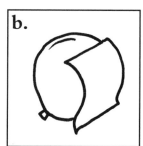

NAME_____

Shadow Shifters

**You can make shadows change.
Get a flashlight and a can.
Turn out the lights.
Then follow each direction below.**

1. Shine the flashlight at the can. Make the longest shadow you can. Draw it here. Be sure to show where the flashlight and the can are, too.

Shadows are made when objects block light.

2. Now make the shortest shadow you can. Draw it here. Be sure to show where the flashlight and the can are.

3. Make the darkest shadow you can. Draw it here. Be sure to show the flashlight and the can.

4. Make the lightest shadow you can. Draw it here. Be sure to show the flashlight and the can.

NAME _____

Mirror, Mirror on the Wall

Leah knows that when she looks in the mirror she sees herself.
She thinks that she will see her reflection in other shiny objects, too.
Is she right?
Do this experiment to find out.

What you need:
- metal pot cover
- pillow
- book
- aluminum foil
- metal spoon
- bottle

What you do:

1. Look in each object. Do you see yourself? If you do, write or draw the object in the space below.

2. Was Leah right about seeing her reflection in shiny objects? How do you know? _____

_____

_____

_____

Around the House: Make a list of other objects that show your reflection.

NAME_____

Read the Clouds

Clouds can tell you what the weather will be.
Read each story.
Look at the clouds in the picture.
Use the information in the chart to answer
the questions.

1. Mike was at the playground. He saw .
   Should he stay and play or go home? _____

   Why do you think so?_____

2. Lisa was leaving for school. She took her umbrella.
   When she got outside she saw

   Will she need her umbrella? _____

   Why do you think so?_____

3. Dion's mother had clothes hanging outside to dry.
   It was a hot day. Dion saw
   Should he bring in the clothes or
   leave them outside? _____

   Why do you think so?_____

Here's a cloud chart	
	Stratus clouds are dark and low in the sky. They bring rain.
	Cirrus clouds are thin and high in the sky. They mean nice weather.
	Cumulus clouds look like white, fluffy cotton balls. When it is hot, they may bring rain. If it is not hot, the weather will be good.

NAME _____

The Water Cycle

The water you drink today may be the same water the dinosaurs drank long ago.
The water cycle makes that possible.
Look at the picture of the water cycle.
Write the letter from the box to show each step of the water cycle.

The water cycle happens over and over again.

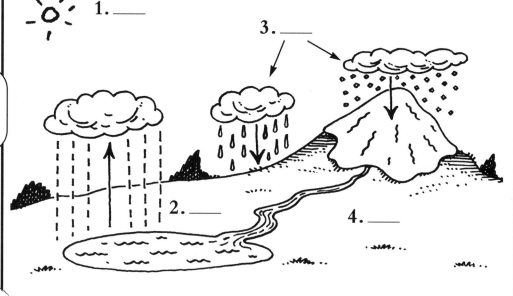

A. The water turns into water vapor. It goes up in the air and becomes clouds.	**B.** The sun warms the water in the lakes and oceans.	**C.** When the water drops get too heavy, they fall down to the ground as rain or snow.	**D.** The rain and snow flows into streams, lakes and oceans.

NAME_____

Water Is Everywhere!

There are tiny water droplets in the air all around you.
How do you know?
Just try this experiment.

What you need:
- a glass jar with a lid
- water
- ice cubes
- a warm place

What you do:
1. Fill the jar with water and ice.
2. Screw on the lid so no water can leak out.
3. Put the jar in a warm place.
4. In 10 minutes, look at the jar. What has changed? Draw a picture of what you see.

When water vapor cools down, it turns back into drops. The cold sides of the jar cooled the air around it. The water vapor in the air turned to drops on the side of the jar. This is called *condensation*.

Around the House: Ask your parents if they know why the sides of cold drinks seem to "sweat" on hot days. Then explain to them what you learned in this experiment.

NAME _____

Around They Go!

Look at the picture of the nine planets and
the sun.
Read the name of each planet.
Use your finger to trace the path of each
planet around the sun.
Then follow the directions on the next page.

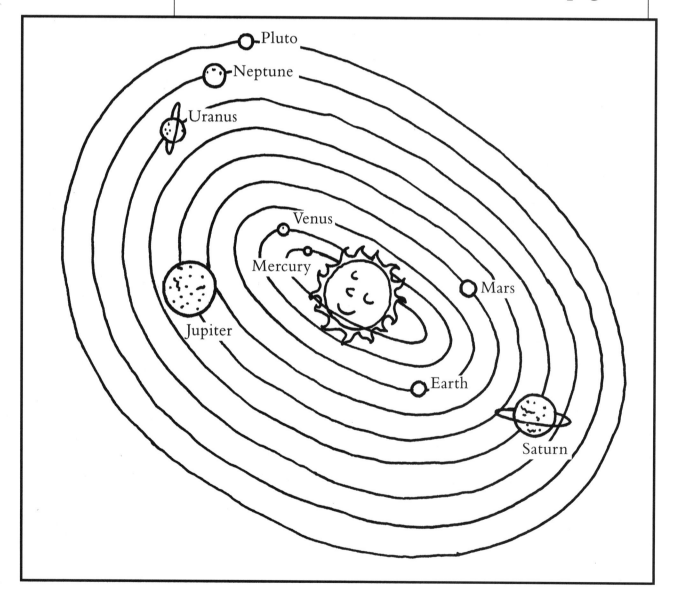

NAME

1. Color the biggest planet brown. Write its name here.

   _____

2. Color the smallest planet yellow. Write its name here.

   _____

3. Circle the planet closest to the sun. Write its name here. _____

4. Put an X on the planet farthest from the sun. Write its name here. _____

5. Color the planet you live on green. Write its name here. _____

6. Color the two planets closest to your planet red. Write their names here. _____

   _____

7. Put a rectangle around the seventh planet from the sun. Write its name here. _____

8. Color the planet with rings blue. Write its name here. _____

The *solar system* is the nine planets and other bodies in the sky that revolve around the sun.

Out of this world! Now cut out the puzzle piece. Glue or tape it in place on page 64.

Around the House: Venus is the brightest object in the sky, besides the sun and the moon. Look for it in the east at sunrise or in the west at sunset.

NAME _____

Day and Night

**Help Dante figure out why it is light in the
day and dark at night.
Use the picture to answer the questions.**

The Earth
rotates, or turns
in place. It
makes a full turn
every 24 hours.
When your side
of the Earth is
turned toward
the sun, you
have daytime.
When it is turned
away from the
sun, you have
night.

Earth

1. Write *day* under the picture of the Earth that shows
   the sun shining on Dante's house.
2. Write *night* under the picture of the Earth that shows
   no sun shining on Dante's house.
3. Why is it light in the day and dark at night? Use the
   pictures above to help you explain this.

   _____

   _____

Around the House: You can see day turn into
night. Watch the sunset on a clear night. Even though it
looks as if the sun is moving, it isn't. The sun stays in one
place. It's the Earth that's really moving.

Technology

Understand
that tools and
machines
solve human
problems

NAME_____

What To Use?

Read each story.
Then look at the pictures of the different machines and tools.
Pick the machine or tool you would use to answer each question.
Write its name on the line.

Tools and machines have parts that move.

Some tools and machines are used for work or to help people solve a problem.

1. You're getting dressed to go outside, but you're not sure what kind of jacket to wear. What would you look at to see how cool it is outside? _____

_____

clock

2. Your suitcase can weigh no more than 30 lbs. to put on the airplane. What can you use to find out whether you can put more things in the suitcase?

_____

paper and pencil

3. The school bus arrives at the same time every day. What can you look at to see if you've missed the bus? _____

_____

scale

4. You're on vacation, and you want to tell your friend back home how you are spending your time. What can you use to send the information? _____

_____

thermometer

Around the House: Look around the house for a tool or machine that helps you do something. What does it help you do?

Grade 2

57

NAME _____

From Tree to Table

These pictures show how people use tools and machines to turn a tree into a table.
Number the pictures from 1 to 6 to show the right order.
Then find and color the tool or machine in each picture.
The first one is numbered for you.

Machines help people make the things they need.

You're a real science machine! Now, put this puzzle piece in the right spot on page 64.

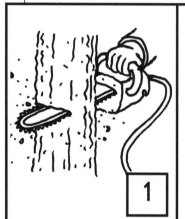
1

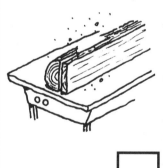

Around the House: Your home is full of machines. How many machines can you find in your kitchen? What does each one do?

GO!

NAME_____

Body Moves

Look at each picture.
Do what each child is doing.
Then find a word from the box that tells what
the child is doing.
Write it on the line.

walking	running	jumping
kicking	throwing	hopping

1. _____

2. _____

3. _____

4. _____

5. _____

6. _____

People can
move their
bodies in
many ways.

Around the House: Try playing a game of "Simon
Says" with friends or family. Tell players to move in
different ways.

NAME _____

See How You Grow

Think about what you were like as a baby.
Think about what you are like now.
Think about what you will be like as a teenager and as an adult.
Draw a picture of yourself at each part of your life.

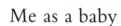

You grow every day. You get bigger in size. You also grow in how you act and think.

Great growing! Now cut out the puzzle piece. Glue or tape it in place on page 64.

Me as a baby

Me as I am right now

Me as a teenager

Me as an adult

Around the House: Find three or four pictures of yourself at different ages. Put them in order. Write a sentence to describe each picture.

NAME_____

Good For You!

Help your family stay healthy.
Make a poster to get your message across.
Circle a topic for your poster.
Then draw your poster in the space below.

Poster topics:

Eat healthy food.   Get enough rest.
Get plenty of exercise.   Keep your body clean.

Around the House: Write down everything you
do for one day. Circle the things that are good for your
health.

NAME _____

Health News

Read the stories below.
Then write the answers to the questions.

1. Carey woke up with a stomachache. He went to the bathroom and threw up. Then his mother took his temperature. Carey had a fever. What should Carey do? _____

_____

_____

_____

Some illnesses, such as colds, chicken pox, and the flu, can spread from one person to another. These illnesses are *contagious*.

2. Gina fell out of a tree. When she landed, she heard something crack in her leg. She screamed in pain. Her dad came running. "I think you broke your leg," he said. What should Gina do? _____

_____

_____

_____

3. Molly was playing soccer. The soccer ball hit her in the head. She got dizzy and fell to the ground. What should Molly do? _____

_____

_____

_____

NAME

Great Foods

Keep track of all the food you eat in one day.
Write or draw it in the boxes.
Use another piece of paper if you need more
room for your pictures.

People need to
eat a balanced
diet to stay
healthy. This
means they need
foods from the
different food
groups.

| Breakfast | Lunch | Dinner | Snacks |

Now fill in the chart.
Put a check in a box for each food you ate.
If you put more checks than there are shaded
boxes, you ate too much of a food.
If you put less checks than there are shaded
boxes, you probably ate too little of a food.

You've done a
great job with
this book.
Now it's time
to finish the
puzzle.
Congratulations!

fats, oils, and sweets										
milk, yogurt, cheese										
meat, chicken, fish, beans, eggs, nuts										
vegetables										
fruit										
bread, cereal, rice, pasta										

Puzzle

Here's where you glue or paste the puzzle pieces you cut out. When you put them all in place, you'll see your secret message.

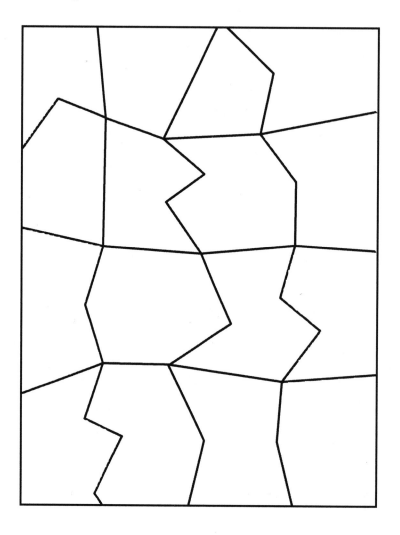

64

Answers

Page 1
Answers will vary.

Page 2

Page 3
Answers will vary. Sample answers: I see trees, birds, squirrels, and flowers. I hear birds chirping. I smell the pine trees and the flowers. I feel the tree bark and the flower petals.

Page 4

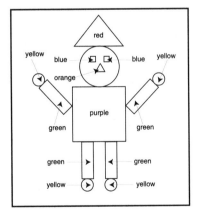

Page 5

Page 6
Living: dog, snake, tree, flower, child
Nonliving: crayon, book, table, pencil, purse

Page 7
1. b
2. a
3. c
4-7 Answers will vary.

Page 8
Results will vary. A leaf usually begins to turn black if it gets no sun.
A plant would die if all its leaves were covered up.

Page 9
1. Color third picture.
2. Color second picture.
3. Color first picture.

Page 10
Forest: oak tree, pine tree, blueberry bushes, bear, deer, bird, raccoon, squirrel
Ocean: fish, starfish, seaweed, sea anemone, crab, lobster, coral

Page 11
Answers will vary. Sample answers: I would pick up the garbage. I would fix the bench. I would clean the lake. I would put out the fire.

Page 12
A. 2
B. 3
C. 4
D. 1

Page 13
1. in soil
2. to get sunlight
3. water
4. Plants need soil, sunlight, and water.

Page 14

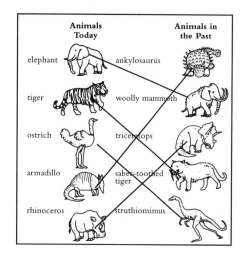

Page 15
1. B
2. F
3. E
4. C
5. D
6. A

Page 16
3. Picture should show ice.
6. Picture should show water boiling and steam rising from water.
7. Water turns to steam.

Page 17
1. yellow
2. blue
3. red
4. blue
5. yellow
6. blue
7. red
8. yellow

Page 18
Sample answers.
2. Thin bands make high, squeaky sounds. Thick bands make deep, low sounds.
4. The sound becomes higher.

Page 19
Red objects: cherries, apple, fire hat, crayon, watermelon, tomato
Round objects: cherries, apple, wheel, ball, ring, plate, balloon, tomato, button, penny
Small objects cherries, pea, ring, button, penny, needle

Page 20
Answers will vary. Sample Answers:
1. road; the other objects are smooth.
2. car; the other objects are soft.
3. ball; the other objects are rough.
4. blanket; the other objects are hard.

Page 21
Answers will vary.

Page 22
The following objects should be circled: nuts, bolts, paper clip, needle, nail, scissors.

Page 23
Answers will vary.

Page 24
1. summer – circle snowman and kid making snow angel.
2. fall – circle woman in lounge, man in shorts.
3. winter – circle flowers, girl flying kite, man mowing.
4. spring – circle girl with skates.

Page 25
Answers will vary.

Page 26
4. The ice cube in the sun melted faster.
5. In the sun, because heat comes from the sun. In the shade the sun is blocked.
6. Harry should cool down in the shade.

Pages 27

Sample answers:

First rock: dark, smallest, rough.

Second rock: small, light, smooth.

Third rock: big, lightest, smoothest.

Pages 28-29

1. tyrannosaurus rex
2. struthiomimus
3. ankylosaurus
4. brachiosaurus

Page 30

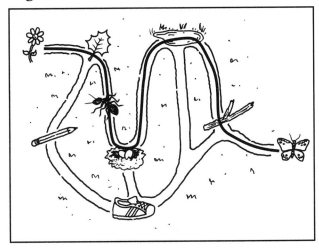

Page 31

2. software
3. disk drive
4. monitor
5. mouse
6. keyboard
7. printer

```
A  B  C  D  D  E  F  G  H  P
M  O  N  I  T  O  R  I  J  R
A  S  K  S  M  Y  Z  A  B  I
C  C  L  K  O  O  C  D  E  N
H  R  M  D  U  X  B  F  G  T
I  E  N  R  S  V  W  S  T  E
N  E  O  I  E  N  L  K  E  R
E  N  P  V  O  P  M  L  Q  Q
Q  R  K  E  Y  B  O  A  R  D
S  O  F  T  W  A  R  E  E  R
```

Page 32

Sample answers:

On Land: bus, train, car, bicycle, truck, roller blades

On Water: ship, rowboat

In the Air: airplane, helicopter, space shuttle

Page 33

X: horse and buggy, child dressed in 1800s clothes, masted ship, steam locomotive

Circle: train, car, modernly-dressed child, cruise ship

Page 34

2. too high
3. O.K.
4. too high

Page 35

4. Picture should show that the plain water froze and the water with salt did not.
5. Maria was right. The salt kept the water from freezing.

Page 36

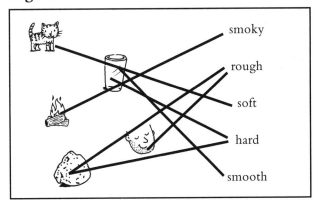

Pages 37

Page 38

Answers will vary, but each boy must have two jobs each.

Page 39

1. piano lessons
2. Wednesday
3. Drawings will vary.

Page 40

1. Thursday, March 4
2. She saw a bird making a nest.
3. Birds make their own homes.
4. Answers will vary. Sample answer: A log helps Sally remember what she sees, does, and learns.

Page 41

1. snake
2. seal
3. bee

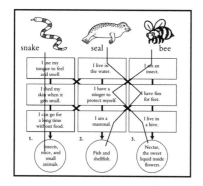

Page 42

1. cactus
2. rattlesnake
3. coyote
4. sagebrush

Page 43

1. mouse
2. owl
3. plant
4. snake

Pages 44–45

Mammals: bear, lion, monkey
Birds: eagle, sparrow, penguin
Reptiles: iguana, rattlesnake, tortoise
Fish: flounder, sawfish, shark

Page 46

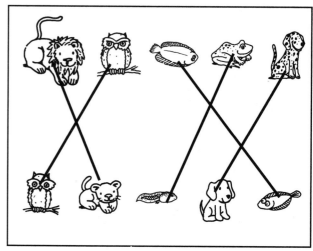

1. Answers will vary. Sample answers: The babies are smaller than the mothers. The puppy doesn't have spots. The cub doesn't have a mane. The tadpole doesn't have legs.
2. Answers will vary. Sample answers: The owls have feathers. The dogs look alike. The fish swim in water and have fins and scales.

Page 47

	Man	Boy
male	√	√
female		
tall	√	
short		√
curly hair	√	
straight hair		√
dark hair	√	
light hair		√
freckles		√
no freckles	√	
glasses	√	
no glasses		√

Page 48
1. b
2. b

Page 49
Answers will vary.

Page 50
1. pot cover, aluminum foil, metal spoon
2. Leah was right. You can see yourself in the shiny objects.

Page 51
1. Go home. Stratus clouds bring rain.
2. No. Cirrus clouds mean fair weather.
3. Bring in the clothes. On a hot day cumulus clouds can bring rain.

Page 52
1. B
2. A
3. C
4. D

Page 53
Answers will vary.

Page 54-55
1. Jupiter
2. Pluto
3. Mercury
4. Pluto
5. Earth
6. Venus and Mars
7. Uranus
8. Saturn

Pages 56
1. Day should be on Earth on the left.
2. Night should be on Earth on the right.
3. The sun shines on Dante's house in the day and doesn't shine on it at night.

Page 57
1. thermometer
2. scale
3. clock
4. paper and pencil

Page 58

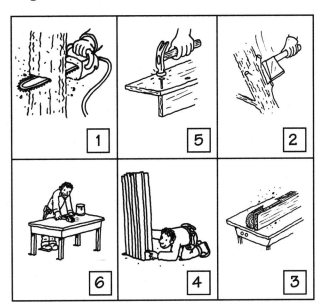

Page 59
1. running
2. jumping
3. throwing
4. walking
5. kicking
6. hopping

Page 60
Answers will vary.

Page 61
Answers will vary.

Page 62
Answers will vary.

Page 63
Each group should be represented at least once at each meal except bread, cereal, rice, and pasta, which should have food to equal a total of 6 to 11 servings. Fats, oils, and sweets should have no more than 1 or 2 servings.

How Do You Foster Your Child's Interest in Learning?

In preparing this series, we surveyed scores of parents on this key question. Here are some of the best suggestions:

- Take weekly trips to the library to take out books, and attend special library events.

- Have lots of books around the house, especially on topics of specific interest to children.

- Read out loud nightly.

- Take turns reading to each other.

- Subscribe to age-appropriate magazines.

- Point out articles of interest in the newspaper or a magazine.

- Tell each other stories.

- Encourage children to write journal entries and short stories.

- Ask them to write letters and make cards for special occasions.

- Discuss all the things you do together.

- Limit TV time.

- Watch selected programs on TV together, like learning/educational channels.

- Provide project workbooks purchased at teacher supply stores.

- Supply lots of arts and crafts materials and encourage children to be creative.

- Encourage children to express themselves in a variety of ways.

- Take science and nature walks.

- Teach children to play challenging games such as chess.

- Provide educational board games.

- Supply lots of educational and recreational computer games.

- Discuss what children are learning and doing on a daily basis.

- Invite classmates and other friends over to your house for team homework assignments.

- Keep the learning experiences fun for children.

- Help children with their homework and class assignments.

- Take trips to museums and museum classes.

- Visits cities of historical interest.

- Takes trips to the ocean and other fun outdoor locations (fishing at lakes, mountain hikes).

- Visit the aquarium and zoo.

- Cook, bake, and measure ingredients.

- Encourage children to participate in sports.

- Listen to music, attend concerts, and encourage children to take music lessons.

- Be positive about books, trips, and other daily experiences.

- Take family walks.

- Let children be part of the family decision-making process.

- Sit down together to eat and talk.

- Give a lot of praise and positive reinforcement for your child's efforts.

- Review child's homework that has been returned by the teacher.

- Encourage children to use resources such as the dictionary, encyclopedia, thesaurus, and atlas.

- Plant a vegetable garden outdoors or in pots in your kitchen.

- Make each child in your family feel he or she is special.

- Don't allow children to give up, especially when it comes to learning and dealing with challenges.

- Instill a love of language; it will expose your child to a richer thought bank.

- Tell your children stories that share, not necessarily teach a lesson.

- Communicate your personal processes with your children.

- Don't talk about what your child did not do. Put more interest on what your child did do. Accept where your child is at, and praise his or her efforts.

- Express an interest in children's activities and schoolwork.

- Limit TV viewing time at home and foster good viewing habits.

- Work on enlarging children's vocabulary.

- Emphasize learning accomplishments, no matter how small.

- Go at their own pace; People learn at different rates.

- Challenge children to take risks.

- Encourage them to do their best, not be the best.